ROCKET SHIP YOGA

YOGA

An Out-of-This-World Kids' Yoga Journey for Breathing, Relaxing and Mindfulness

ROCKET SHIP YOGA

An Out-of-This-World Kids' Yoga Journey for Breathing, Relaxing and Mindfulness

BARI KORAL

ACCLAIMED CHILDREN'S MUSIC ARTIST AND KIDS' YOGA EXPERT

CORAL GABLES

Cover Design: Kim Balacuit
Illustrations: Bari Koral
Layout & Design: Kim Balacuit

Rocket Ship Yoga: An Out-of-This-World Kids' Yoga Journey for Breathing, Relaxing and Mindfulness

Library of Congress Cataloging-in-Publication number: 2021952728
ISBN: (print) 978-1-64250-860-4, (ebook) 978-1-64250-861-1
BISAC category code JNF013110, JUVENILE NONFICTION / Concepts / Body

Printed in the United States of America

INTRODUCTION

From social media to busy schedules and uncertain times, our little ones are showing more signs of stress than ever before.

There is a bright side: we can use this time to build resilience in our children (and in ourselves) and to better learn to ride the ups and downs of life.

Imagine a world where children have the power to calm and soothe themselves from an early age.

Let's create that world now.

The book you have in your hands will enable you to help the children around you. Featuring engaging yoga, guided relaxation, and breathing, our rocket ship yoga adventure gives children precious tools they can use anywhere, anytime they want to feel calmer and safer.

As we go through our space journey, our bodies will become stronger, more flexible, and better able to unwind and let go.

You can use this book regularly and feel free to level up. Simply slow down the poses and breathe three to five times in each pose. (More on this in the glossary.)

Let's blast off to a better future together, starting now!

Love, Bari

Before we blast off, let's warm up with Rocket Ship Breath!

Sit up tall and let your spine be long.

Close your eyes.

Inhale slowly, and imagine your breath lifting up toward the sky. This is your rocket lifting off into space.

Pause for 5, 4, 3, 2, 1.

Exhale slowly and imagine your breath lowering back down. This is your rocket landing safely back on Earth.

Try this 3-5 times.

I wanted to be a pilot
ever since I was a child.

CHILD'S POSE

Sit back on your heels.

Bring your forehead to the floor.

Rest both arms along the sides of your body.

Tip: Take 3–5 deep breaths.

I would gaze up at the stars looking for Mars.

SNAKE POSE

Lie on your belly.

Place your hands flat on the floor by your shoulders and slowly lift up your chest while you gaze at the stars.

Let your legs be as long as a snake!

Tip: Take 3-5 slow, calming breaths.

I could fly a big rocket
and go far into orbit.

PLANK POSE

Start on your hands and knees.

Place your shoulders over your wrists. Walk your legs back and raise them off the floor.

Your body should be a long straight line, like a plank—or a big rocket!

Press your hands and legs strongly into the earth.

Tip: Try to hold for 30 seconds to 1 minute. Put your knees down to modify.

Blast into space to see what awaits.

DOWNWARD DOG

Start on your hands and knees.

Press your hands flat and keep them firmly on the floor.

Stretch your legs back, tuck in your toes, and lift your hips to the sky.

Let your arms and legs be strong.

I land with a boom

And walk on the moon.

From Downward Dog,

take several steps forward and back

to walk on the moon!

I jump through the air
To feel gravity there.

DONKEY KICKS

From downward dog, press your arms strongly into the ground.

Bend your knees and take a few donkey kicks.

Watch your body and make sure no one is behind you as you kick!

After some donkey kicks, jump or walk your feet to your hands.

As my feet touch the ground,

I explore what's around.

STANDING FORWARD BEND

Stand with your feet hip-width apart and fold forward at the waist.

Let your head drop toward the floor. Your hands may land on the ground or dangle down.

Gently sway from side to side as you explore the ground in outer space!

Tip: Keep a slight bend in your knees.

EXTENDED MOUNTAIN POSE

Stand tall. Press your legs
firmly into the ground.

Inhale and stretch your arms
strongly up toward the sky.

Stretch back slightly for a nice
opening backbend.

I reach up to the sky
where it's dark, with no light.

CRESCENT MOON POSE

Stand tall with your feet together.

Interlace your fingers and point
your index fingers up.

Keep your feet strong on the ground
and raise your torso up to the sky.

Stretch to one side of the sky,
so you can touch the moon!

Tip: Take 3-5 breaths on one side
before bending to the other side.

I touch one side of the moon.

Switch sides in crescent moon pose.

And the other side too.

I have come all this way on my own.

I'm not heading home.

MOUNTAIN POSE

Stand tall. Press your legs firmly into the ground.

Let your spine be long, with your head
reaching up toward the sky.

Press your arms firmly into prayer hands.
Stay rooted in the ground like a strong mountain!

Tip: Stay here for 1 minute and take
some slow, deep breaths.

FROG POSE

Stand with your legs hip-distance apart.

Turn your feet out slightly, if comfortable. Squat down.

Gently push your knees apart with your elbows.

I'm ready to launch.

Hold your squat for a few moments and then count:

5, 4, 3, 2, 1—BLAST OFF!

and prepare to blast off.

WARRIOR 3 POSE

Press one leg strongly into the ground.
Lift one leg up into the air and fly!

To help keep your balance, pick a
spot to gaze at on the floor.

Use a wall to balance if you need to.

I fly out, out to outer space...

35

further and further and further away...

Switch sides. Press the opposite leg strongly into the ground. Bring your other leg up into the air and fly!

Now I touch all the stars.

STAR POSE

Step your feet wide apart and stretch your arms out to the sides.

Take some deep breaths and feel your energy expand out through your toes and fingers.

Gently lift one leg to balance in your star pose.

Repeat Star Pose on the other side.

I'm the first to touch Mars.

Ssshhh...

There's not a sound in the place!

Everything is so quiet in space.

LET'S PLAY THE LISTENING GAME

Sit crisscross or in a comfortable seat on the ground.

With your eyes closed, just listen to what
is around you for one minute.

Ssssh—just listen.

When you are ready, open your eyes.

Now I lay on my back
To watch the stars swirl...

SHAVASANA: RESTING POSE

From my new place
in this world.

Lie on your back or somewhere you are comfortable. Take a few breaths in and out. Let your body relax and let go after your outer space adventure. Notice how you feel.

Stay here for a minute or longer.

Let's end our space adventure with Star Relaxation

(read slowly, taking time to pause after each line)

Close your eyes and imagine a sky full of stars.

Now reach your arms up, up, up and grab a star right out of the sky.

Close your hands and now start to rub your hands together quickly.

Keep rubbing your hands faster and faster, so you can feel the warmth of your star (rub for at least 10 seconds).

Now, stop rubbing.

Gently start to pull your hands apart.
Can you feel the heat of your star?
You might even feel your hands tingling.
Feel the energy in your hands from your star.

Now you can place your hands on your heart
and rub your heart gently with the warmth of
your star. Your heart feels warm and happy.

When you are ready, open your eyes.

THE END

GLOSSARY: HOW TO USE THIS BOOK

This book is set up similarly to a yoga class. We have a warm-up (our rocket ship breath), then we do a main movement (our rocket ship adventure), and then we rest and relax (star relaxation).

While yoga increases strength, stamina, flexibility, and more, the ultimate goal of yoga is to prepare us to relax. The systematic forward bending, back bending, stretching, twisting, and core work (all contained in our book) help the body let go.

Postures like **Rocket Ship Stretch** open up the chest cavity, increasing the capacity for more breath. This oxygen aids in bringing on the relaxation response of our parasympathetic nervous system.

Children, especially our younger children, will be excited about our rocket ship yoga adventure and may initially want to fly through the book. That's fine—have fun!

But as you return to the book throughout the year, here is how to level it up: Simply, slow it down.

Work toward staying with each pose for 3-5 breaths. Take your time. Inhale and exhale completely.

As you start to slow down and practice breathing, you will see big changes in the behavior, focus, and attention span of your children.

These practices give children the power to self-regulate, focus and reduce stress.

Practice the rocket ship adventure along with your children. When you breathe in and out, breathe with them. Model slow, deep breaths. This book is for your benefit, too.

POSE GALLERY

Here are some additional benefits to each yoga pose.

CHILD'S POSE

• **Benefits:** Relaxes the muscles on the front of the body and opens the hips in a very gentle way. Encourage children to feel the connection to the ground as they rest.

• **Modify:** For children three and under, this pose may look a little different. You can encourage them to sit back on their heels and find a pose where they can be "resting." After some practice, they will be able to do a full Child's Pose.

SNAKE POSE

- **Benefits:** Improves flexibility and stretches the shoulders, chest, and belly.

- **Modify:** Depending on age and flexibility, some children might be able to lift their chest up higher.

PLANK POSE

• Benefits: Tones all the core muscles including the belly, chest, and lower back. Strengthens the arms, wrists, and shoulders.

• Tip: The positioning in Plank Pose is the top of a push-up. As children get tired, they can release their legs to the floor and come to their hands and knees. You can encourage them to keep their belly lifted to get the full benefits.

DOWNWARD DOG

• **Benefits:** Stretches hamstrings, shoulders, calves, arches, hands, and spine while building strength in arms, shoulders, and legs.

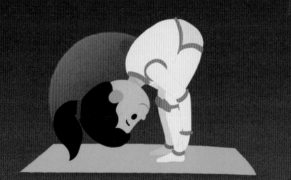

STANDING FORWARD BEND (RAGDOLL POSE)

• **Benefits:** Strengthening and stretching the calves and hamstrings. Releases tension in the back.

EXTENDED MOUNTAIN POSE

- **Benefits:** Boosts energy and expands the chest and the rib cage, resulting in more oxygen intake. Tones the organs of the abdomen, improving digestion.

CRESCENT MOON/STANDING HALF-MOON POSE

• **Benefits:** Tones entire leg muscles and hips, increases flexibility of the upper body, and builds concentration.

MOUNTAIN POSE

- **Benefits:** Improves posture, balance, and focus.

FROG POSE/SQUAT

• **Benefits:** Increases flexibility in the hips, releases the lower back.

• **Tip:** For more of a challenge, try to balance in this pose. Have children place their hands together at the center of their heart and sit up straight in Frog Pose.

WARRIOR 3/AIRPLANE POSE

• **Benefits:** Improves balance and coordination and strengthens leg, back, and core muscles.

• **Tip:** To begin the pose, find a spot on the floor and focus on it. This will help you establish your balance.

BALANCING STAR POSE

· Benefits: An energizing pose that tests core strength and balance while lengthening the body in all directions at once.

THE LISTENING GAME

- **Benefits:** Increases focus, concentration, and present-moment awareness.

- **Modify:** Once children have mastered the skill of listening for one full minute, acknowledge their success and offer the challenge of playing the listening game for two minutes, or even longer.

- **Tip:** Vary the game and listen to just human sounds (breathing, coughing, etc.) or non-human sounds (air conditioner, wind, etc.).

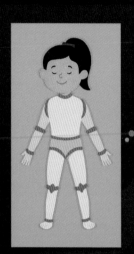

SHAVASANA/FINAL RESTING POSE

• **Benefits:** Calms central nervous system, aids digestive and immune systems.

• **Tip:** Here, the many benefits of our yoga practice integrate while we lay down and rest. We work to relax physical and mental tension and let go of what we don't need in this moment.

ABOUT THE AUTHOR

Bari Koral is a beloved children's recording artist and an internationally recognized kids yogi. Every day, tens of thousands of parents and teachers use her music, instruction, and tools with young children. Bari has been called a "kids yoga pioneer" (Kaplan Early Learning Company). Her popular "Bari Koral" kids yoga, music and mindfulness Youtube channel serves millions of teachers, parents, and children.

After Bari's personal ten-year battle with stress and anxiety, she has dedicated her life to educating others about the powerful tools she discovered. Bari has presented on the benefits of yoga and mindfulness to over 100,000 teachers (and counting). She has been a keynote speaker at the nation's top educational conferences.

She has performed numerous times at the White House and has been featured in *People Magazine* and *The New York Times*. Yogapalooza: Yoga and Mindfulness with Bari Koral is RCYS Registered Children's Yoga School with Yoga Alliance. She lives in Saugerties, New York, with her husband and two children. This is her first book. For more information, visit Bari's website: barikoral.com.

DragonFruit, an imprint of Mango Publishing, publishes high-quality children's books to inspire a love of lifelong learning in readers. DragonFruit publishes a variety of titles for kids, including children's picture books, nonfiction series, toddler activity books, pre-K activity books, science and education titles, and ABC books. Beautiful and engaging, our books celebrate diversity, spark curiosity, and capture the imaginations of parents and children alike.

Mango Publishing, established in 2014, publishes an eclectic list of books by diverse authors. We were named the Fastest-Growing Independent Publisher by Publishers Weekly in 2019 and 2020. Our success is bolstered by our main goal, which is to publish high-quality books that will make a positive impact in people's lives.

Our readers are our most important resource; we value your input, suggestions, and ideas. We'd love to hear from you—after all, we are publishing books for you!

Please stay in touch with us and follow us at:
Instagram: @dragonfruitkids
Facebook: Mango Publishing
Twitter: @MangoPublishing
LinkedIn: Mango Publishing
Pinterest: Mango Publishing

Sign up for our newsletter at www.mangopublishinggroup.com and receive a free book! Join us on Mango's journey to change publishing, one book at a time.